Overthought Thoughts
of a 21-Year-Old

By: Angela Prendergast

Late Night Views

12:58am

There is something so magical about the nighttime when all is asleep.

Creak. The floor boards whisper to the lavender wallpaper, leaving the paper to curl with laughter in the dewy summer air.

Dong. The grandmother clock reminds the ceiling fan of a hilarious memory from a past night; a secret safe between the two.

Swoosh. The fan laughs at the charming storyteller clock, responding in covert exchange.

When everyone is sleeping, things seem different. I look at furniture in different shapes and colors. I find a steady comfort in the items which occupy my room. I salute the guitar which will come to life in the morning with boisterous energy and vibrating strings.

I make peace and reconcile with the thoughts that occupy my brain. Let them leave my mind and bounce off the indigo façade that shades me from the outdoors.

I am safe in my room.

I take comfort in my small four corners, adorned with familiar features that will be there to greet me in the dawn of the day.

I fall asleep, thanking these possessions for still being with me when the sun rises. Thanks for never leaving.

Distance vs. Miles

1:13am

I feel closer to you when we are apart, for when we are close enough to touch, our distance can't be measured by miles, but rather a unit of much greater width.

Loose

1:17am

We are loose shoelaces; meant to be held together for safety, but instead fall free with every stumble.

Nostalgia of the Anonymous

3:00am

How can you miss something you never had?

A surely acute feeling, to miss something you have never experienced.

How can you put together the heart you didn't break?

Hibernation

12:32am

Does the bear miss the sun when he goes into hibernation? Or does he simply free his mind of the way the sun felt? Maybe he never really felt the sun's rays, and that is why he sleeps so soundly in its absence.

The Crash

2:44am

You were a meteorite crashing into my heart.

Exploding the small muscle with a fire so enormous,

dust and ash covered the insides. You set forth an

impact winter after the attack. The same fiery warmth

felt on collision, turned to an icy sting. The prolonged

cold shattered that same fiery muscle into tiny little

pieces. After emerging with such an explosion, I

should have known you could not be trusted.

A Sad Epiphany

6:00pm

I miss yesterday today. I'll miss today tomorrow. I'll miss tomorrow forever because I've overlooked every tomorrow worrying about the next.

Which I'd Prefer...

4:02am

Sometimes the night keeps me from sleeping and sometimes sleeping keeps me from the night.

I cannot tell which I'd rather prefer.

11:07am

Her heart cried out for something, but for what
her brain was unsure.

I'll get around to it

8:11am

As the sun begins to rise, it creeps in my room, illuminating the messy pile of clothes in my closet. I cringe at the sight... reaching for the string to pull the blinds shut. Darkness returns. Much better. I hate staring at that cluttered mess. I must clean the closet. Most of the clothes outgrew me anyway.

Permit Required

2:15am

You pop into my mind from time to time. You are not welcome in my safe haven. Don't you know it's illegal to trespass?

Making one out of two

6:14pm

I had to detach from you to show my full potential,

the concept of my self-worth is beyond essential.

Now I sit back and watch you take the stage alone.

We are each other, in essence, down to the skin and bone.

We will forever remain strangers,

due to things we said out of anger.

Everything Left In-Between

11:12pm

I figured out why I like getting up in the morning and going to bed at night. It is because the start and finish are easy. It's the turbulence in-between that weights me to the earth.

The Beauty in Uncertainty

11:33pm

Your experiences at this age are meant to be messy. They are meant to be jumbled and clouded and overwhelmingly catastrophic. Embracing the beauty in uncertainty is what youth is about!

6:13pm

Write. Write to work out the kinks in your head. Write until the cramping of your hand substitutes the distress and pain in your heart, and then write some more.

Release Me

1:48am

I just want to have fun. I want freedom from all chains; mainly the ones in my mind.

717 Nights

12:05am

Happiness is... twenty toes tangled together in delight.

Happiness is... the permanent stain you marked on my heart.

Happiness is... the catalyst of your being.

Happiness is... the uniform consistency of our two hearts beating as one.

Circa 2015

The grass is always green... you just need to stand in the right light to see it.

Route 999

We are two highways running parallel to one another. We dart together in the night, occasionally meeting for a short sequence of time. We race side by side, never stopping at the bend. We bear right, left and circle in the light of the moon. We zoom too close together at the curve, resulting in a dead end. You move forward with a quick zig-zag motion and dash on, never to meet again.

3:14pm

Too far away for me to hold, too close enough for me to clutch.

10:33pm

I'M TIRED OF MY OPINIONS. LET ME DRINK UP YOUR SWEET APPREHENSIONS FOR THE NIGHT.

12:34am

Why do I seek approval from those I do not know? Why do I disregard praise from those who matter most?

Guitars

1:00am

Pluck your fingers against the strings of my heart,

play me a melody ensuring we'll never part.

21st Century Problems

7:12pm

If my Instagram photos can't grasp your attention, than surely my success will. Thanks for the motivation.

Find what you are passionate about and fire it up. Light a flame that burns down the East and West Coast.

12:06pm

Find something that makes you feel alive,

and die for it.

Mosaic Arrangements

3:17am

When things are broken they are even more immensely beautiful. When something is left in fragments, the pieces stand independent from the final product as a whole. Those disconnected divisions make you human. Those disconnected divisions make you.... You.

I'm drowning in three feet of water. I'm 5'10. I think I forgot how to stand.

Your heart remembers the things your brain forgets.

Waves of the Ocean

5:07pm

Pull me in. Drag me towards you with a force I cannot fall free from. Toss me around, bent backward, and flipped on my side. Push me away, leave me dumped towards the shore to lay helpless, my body scratched and deconstructed from the sand. My waves of the ocean.

Sleeping on Stones

2:55am

Toss and turn in bed.

Must escape from my head.

I turn one way and it hurts my back,

Try another position and my body falls out of whack.

This mattress feels like pins and tacks,

Or maybe I need to learn to be comfortable where I am at.

Stay as Long as You Need.

6:00am

Your words bleach my ears. Your touch thrashes my skin.

Yet, your beauty continues to ease my eyes. Please stay.

Never Lost but Forever Found

1:12am

I was never lost. Just
instinctively diverting my
footsteps in your direction.
Thanks for matching the pace of my
strides and being my imperishable
destination.

Whole

1:18am

Hold me tight and love me.

No, hold me, just hold me.

If things get complicated and my equilibrium cannot be recovered, you can let go. In fact, let go if you want to. I know I will still be here for myself and that is all I need.

At Ease

11:11pm

Your smile pushes me to forgive the places I have been, and forget the places I will be. In this moment, I am with you.

Questions Beyond Me

3:29am

Why does everything filled with life get taken away so quickly?

Why does everything lacking life get to live forever?

Time

8:09pm

Time: The ultimate instigator to all my worries.

The cackle in the back of my mind as I drift to sleep. The itch in my psyche as I burden my thoughts with tomorrow.

The tear in my heart as I reflect on how much it has stolen from me.

The throbbing pain in my back as I realize how I have stretched myself thin for it.

The suffocating presence of it as I think of the days I have been pressed for it.

Time: The always present problem and never ending solution.

Dulling the Diamond

10:10pm

I myself am morphing; frightened that I have begun to lack luster.

Yet, the old version of myself, I do not trust her.

Mold, shape, outline; contour my silhouette into perfect form.

Watch out! Pay mind to the signs preaching warn.

I may no longer sparkle in silver and gold,

But it is my dignity of which I uphold.

4:37am

My biggest flaw is wanting love from those who are least capable of giving it.

Keep Out

1:20am

The more I leave the door open, the more opportunities for danger to sneak into my home. I keep the blinds shut and the knob locked.　　　　There is no open door policy here.

Mislead

9:55pm

You bring me the most vibrant and
abstract flowers, so soft and
easy on the eyes, only to throw
them in my coffin and lay them
atop my grave.

Lows and Highs

2:22am

I am on a sliding scale moving swiftly back and forth. It sways between absolute elation and complete abjection.

A ride I want off.

Passing in Brief

11:19pm

The night brings a tender passing of a warm breath of wind, wafting through the midnight sky.

It melts through the trees quickly, touching them for a brief moment, only to proceed to the next.

So gently in the way it approaches, playing the branches like the strings of a cello.

A master of manipulation, no stranger to the shining of an apple.

Once it has finished passing through, the branches stop blowing. The warm passing continues on in the night, not bothering to look back at the impact it made.

Boundaries

1:00am

Draw a line between who you are
and who you once were; a boundary
which should be clear and
uncrossed. Be conscious of what
lies on either side of that line.

Note the differences. You are not
your past.

What's stretched across an artist's wooden frame?
12:14am

She is a piece of THE blank canvas, waiting to be etched out. For even the most abstract, amateur combination of uncorrelated colors splashed on the page would be more beautiful than the nothingness which currently occupies her.

Revolution

11:39pm

Your **rejection** gave me the greatest sense of self-resurrection,

reflection and *resolution*. I am the leader of my own REVOLUTION.

Like Moths to a Smile

12:52am

He says, "turn **off** the light when it gets dark. The moths will cloud my vision and I would much rather sit in the darkness than have to view those revolting creatures." I proceed to turn **on** the light, even daring to open the window.

I politely reply, "The light welcomes their distaste with fortitude. Don't you know the counterparts complement each other?" Nothing. I speak another language to him.

"Forgetting" you….

1:11am

How much longer must I push away the thought of you?

I admit, this very thought is what lies heavily behind my eyelids at night.

Visions in Honda Mirrors

4:48pm

For a split second a vision appeared in my rear-view. It looked queerly familiar, or rather felt familiar. A moment, a rush of longing, so tangible it could have been crushed between the slender gaps in my fingers. A hunger for the simple essence of the image behind me. Momentarily, the image disappeared almost as quickly as it entered, leaving behind a bleakness for the past that shuffled around my nostalgic thoughts. Each exhale moved me farther away from the vision in the rear-view. I drove faster.

Don't Overthink

2:20pm

Every minute detail sinks into our pores, complicating every inch of our flesh. Combat this. Keep love simple.

Free

3:30am

Emancipate yourself from the chambers of fear within your heart.

Never let doubt bite your tongue, slit your veins, or staple your wings.

For Your Records

11:50pm

I am your personal tape recorder; forever memorizing your words and committing each conversation to memory, matching up the sentences on a rainy day.

Life be Long

10:58pm

Today I experienced a dominant and acute feeling that life was starting over and happiness was near. A strong vitality which kept me from hoping life be short.

My heart is messy and stained. Don't try to sterilize me from my faults. It is these natural and organic defects that make me pure.

Move

2:09am

I'm terrified by the idea of being paralyzed. Paralyzed, that is, by the vices of this vicious world. I will not be confined and comfortable with a motionless existence. I will stand for life.

The Promise

12:19am

I promise I will not retreat back to what is comfortable. Even if a situation appears vexatious, I will keep stumbling through the madness, simply with the goal of having a lot to talk about on my death bed.

Dizzy

Things are good! Things are bad. Now it's back to the circle.

I'm sucked into the vicious whirlpool of life. Flailing arms, dizzy visions, blurred lines, spinning mind, spinningg minndd,

sppiiinniiiiinnnngggggg miiinnndddd.

Renovations

2:12am

We paint the shutters a new color.

We open the blinds to soak in the sun's rays.

I smile. Right here is where I choose to stay.

I move beyond my old ways.

We have become each other's home,

from which I will never roam.

Temporary

1-3:00pm

With every fleeting moment of happiness, I wait for the boundless minutes of gloom. I watch the clock.

1 o'clock brings me fresh fruit of vibrant colors.

3 o'clock finds them decayed. Tick-Tock.

Stunning Ruins

11:45pm

Do not use glue on your heart,

Let the pieces break apart.

When you're down and the fragments pull away from each other,

Is when vulnerability lets you discover your special lover.

Allow your soul to collapse and shatter to the ground.

For it is in this instance that the purest love can be found.

Adorn

12:07am

Decorate me with the vibrant colors of your **past**.

Let every stroke of paint show me a future built to **last**.

Pay No Mind

6:19pm

Please don't pay my existence any mind,

As I sulk under a tree, wallowing, wasting my time.

The leaves dance to the wind's melody in C minor,

As my mind imagines infeasible ways to become finer.

Tears

1:43am

Engulfed by childhood dreams and present day fears... I am ashamed of this hot, salty substance falling down my cool cheeks. I am wretchedly familiar with this sting falling from the green mirrors of my soul.

Dreams in the Dirt

8:55pm

The birds have fell silent.

I can no longer hear a sound,

other than my dreams lying concussed

on the naked ground.

Birds and Gills

7:55pm

The birds fly above me. Each following one another in a circular motion. One falls far behind, flapping its wings in a slow, lethargic way.

He is crying for help. No one hears.

He doesn't want to fly, but learned to keep up his duties.

Perhaps he wants to swim? A surely absurd thought, a black bird swimming in the sea with golden fish. Why shouldn't the bird have such an option?

Surely he'd drown, but how freeing to break from the mold and defy expectations? Flying has provided a deathless death, a lifeless life.

His black feathers, stained by water, glisten. His lungs gasp for air. He realizes in his final demise, he has lived.

Brash Silence

12:00am

There was a lot that needed to be said;
however, the silence was much too clamorous
to compete with. We will try again later.

Good talk.

Selfish?

12:33am

I wonder if we ever really miss people, or rather just miss the feeling we receive from them? Is this a selfish perspective if it is one that all humans occupy?

Solar System

1:02am

You are the moon and I am the sun.

                    We chase each other in never ending concentric circles,

never steadying our paths long enough to exist as one.

Moving Along

7:14am

Last night I took a road trip around our memories. Just east of enjoyment, west of wanderlust, and slightly slipping south towards sadness, ending in the final destination of regret. Next time, I'll take a plane to avoid the pointless stops along the way.

The Comatose.

2:59am

I want to cut myself off. Tear myself from

the toxic feelings that cling relentlessly

onto my every being. Rip myself from the

black smoke engulfing my mind, clouding

my breath. Provide me an excuse to empty

myself for a minute. Comatose.

The Formation of a Backbone

2:35pm

I refuse to apologize for refusing to apologize. I have a voice of a song bird, with a melody from the heart. You are a parrot, simply mimicking the tunes of another.

Boats in the Distance

12:47am

Why let anyone sail into our lives if the wind will just blow them away from us in time?

I will be the captain of my own ship and steer blindly, quietly through the night, with the hopes of never crashing into another.

Opportunities

11:49pm

My biggest fear is not that God won't respond to my prayers, but rather that I won't seize the prayers he responds to.

Dance

I danced. Wildly, moving my hips and waving my arms.

Synchronizing my movements with the light pulse of the music.

I danced to remember.

I danced to be present, here and now.

Becoming one with the melody, I melted away,

Emptying my intellect temporarily and continuing on,

Floating away with the sounds.

What a wonderful feeling it is, to be

Reminiscent, yet unmindful all in the same motion.

Stage Five Clinger

3:55 am

I'm suffocated by loneliness. Loneliness is a clingy friend that I cannot seem to escape from. Why so smothering? I want it to leave me alone.

Painting a Portrait

6:45am

I decorate myself every morning by pounding nails into my flesh and hanging up portraits of my deepest regrets. I drape on heavy coats of self-doubt and vacillation.

I paint my porcelain skin with uncertainty, accompanied by the warmest color of anxiety.

And yet, through all this discomfort, the most painful thing to plaster on in accordance with the rising sun, is a smile.

Sanity

8:00pm

In a world muddled with madness, I

made a conscious effort to stay sane.

The Long End of the Stick

3:22pm

I politely decline your avid
attempts to mold me into you,
    a fight you will never win.
Nothing against you,
    but I was not built to blend in.

A Pleasure to Meet You?

9:08pm

Who is this real world fellow and why does everyone keep talking about him as if he's the big bad wolf lurking in the forest?

Why does the description of this real world character change with every age I grow into?

He is infamous. Will I ever meet real world? I have heard the nasty rumors about him, and I don't know if I want to shake his hand.

Watch and Never Learn

Circa 2015

I fear I am destined to observe and

never experience.

Stained Feathers

12:48am

I can see the proud, astute silhouette of who I could

be,

but swiftly float farther from the image, as more

shadows appear behind me.

They creep in my vision, overpower my pride,

Stain my white feathers, provide no place to hide.

Another angel chased away by the demons' crowd,

For I cannot overpower them, their presence is far too

loud.

Shimmering Gold

8:22pm

The pigment of your skin approaches and appears as a gold warmth, illuminating any room on entry. You paint the room with your colors everywhere you go. Keep walking in my direction.

The Death of a Party

It appears I am at a party,
but inside my head, there is a
funeral welcomed by
contemptuous thoughts.
            The boisterous
screams and music push me
    deeper into my mind.

They might as well start
playing the taps now.

A House and a Home

12:33am

I regret defining home in a tangible way. It is not something I can see or touch.

I regret giving you the authority and responsibilities of being my home.

Now, I know that home is wherever I am. Home is sacred and within me.

A Broken Leg on a Marble Floor

2:16am

My hands and feet keep slipping on this rocky surface,

A surface I have been occupying for far too long.

Dense air surrounds, stealing breath,

wrapping its hands in a tight grasp around my neck.

Quick short inhales.

Life seems to be my biggest fail.

Tomorrow, I Leave

2:03am

I am going away for a while.

Do not try and follow.

It seems as though everyone desires something from me,

I may start charging a visitation fee.

I cannot please every single soul,

Leaving me stranded to climb out of this gaping hole.

Therefore, I am taking off in delight,

And jumping on the quickest flight.

Listen with your Eyes.

11:55am

You are a beautiful song to see, a breathtaking sight to hear.

Autumn

5:06pm

I do not trust the purple and blue leaves of October that plummet to the ground in their death.

They mislead me. How is it they manage to look so striking as they fall from life?

I do not trust such a scene that blinds my eyes with great delicacy, only to leave me saddened by the fragility in their demise.

I do not trust.

A Trip around the Track

6:19pm

Run. Run.

Run away.

Run from the past.

Quick! It is catching up!

Run from the future... It is approaching too fast.

The breeze beats my face and thrashes across my hair.

I scream "catch me, catch me....if you **dare**!"

Reciprocate

8:47pm

The hands of a clock get bored as they circle from 5 to 6, from 9 to 10. A constant state that will forever reciprocate. A continuous, fruitless action bound to repeat in wearisome solitude.

Lavender Stripes

1:03pm

WHY DOES the wallpaper keep LAUGHING AT ME WITh ITS STuPID lavender stripes and ASSUMING HUMOR? WHO GAVE YOU THE AUTHORITY to view all my MISTAKES AND PAtR0NIZE my FLeSH UPON VIEW?

Tell it to STOP MAKiNg FUn OF ME 0R I'LL PEEL IT OFF THE WALL quicker than it can repeat the wOrD WORTHLESS. FORGIVE ME FOR BEING impolite.

I miss....

1:43am

The things that make me miss you are the same things that I miss within myself. Happiness, sincerity, a familiar face, an abiding warmth. I guess I put too much of myself into you. If this is the case, who do I really miss more?

Proud

2:17pm

Look at you, you remarkable human, you.

You have managed to walk through fire as if the ambers that lashed your arms were merely raindrops invigorating your skin.

You have learned to open yourself to those who are the most closed.

You have hung your lantern in front of those who only see black;

A beacon in the night.

You wore glasses, prescribing prescriptions to those who could not see.

You played monkey-in-the-middle with your feelings and learned how to mediate them.

You loved when you received hate, and continued to love after experiencing such animosity.

You've felt pain in a numb world,

And you have done so all while stimulating your surroundings with your presence.

Look at you. ☺

Take Care

12:13am

Forgiveness unties and unwraps hate from the heart.

Focus not only on forgiveness of others, but also realize you are under complete obligation to forgive yourself.

My Apology

2:02am

I am sorry that all I appear to be doing is complaining, but my life is crying and these pages are the only ones who will listen.

Missed Calls

9:22am

Saturday night left me a voicemail. He spoke that we are over and never getting back together. I wept as I will no longer dance under his beautiful moon and sing of supreme bliss.

I tell myself it is for the best. For as much ecstasy as I received in the moment from Saturday's presence, I found nothing more agonizing than the lectures of Sunday morning.

Notice

3:43pm

I walked outside, a bit startled at first to see the sun shining so brilliantly, truly lambent in appearance.

"Wow, it is so nice out."

His retort, "It has been beautiful all week, you are just noticing this now?"

Smile

4:50pm

Flip your enemies a smile rather than a scowl. It will confuse their insides. ☺

Savanna

1:12am

There must be some middle ground between the gorgeous mountain tops and low rivers for which we can stand.

Every high keeps us cringing and waiting for the low. Every low finds us begging for the next high. Let us wait for the middle ground where we can permanently lie.

Light and Dark.

11:33 am

When a colorful mind meets a dark past, let the unexpected be expected. Look out!

Me Searching for the Depth in You……

1:45am

Throwing a pebble to the wind and telling it to swim.

Requirements

4:00pm

"I miss you too."

Pause.

We both could hear the requirement in your voice.

I Feel

11:20am

I feel uneven today. Like half my body is stronger than the other. Like I'm draped in wet clothes, three sizes too big.

I feel off balance today, like I shouldn't trust the shoes on my feet to keep me planted steady on the ground.

Vs.

12:20am

My sober appearance introduces me to the world as an unassuming human being;

while inside, my drunken thoughts taunt my madness and send this appearance fleeing for the hills.

Bull in the China Shop

3:44am

To be able to sleep so soundly amongst the stridency, clutter, and commotion crooning in your mind is true talent.

Self-love

11:46pm

You are a beautiful rose on your own.

Decorate your petals, independently.

It isn't until then that the other seeds will rise from the dirt to say hello.

I am Proud of YOU

3:45pm

You have had darkness steal your light,

You have had hunger pick at the vegetation of your soul,

And yet, you still manage to keep your smile curved to the sky and your left following your right.

You are amazing.

Grown Cautious

1:30am

I have learned to be wary of living to feel alive.

Permanent Jewelry

2:08am

She wore her new bracelets as a martyr. A flashy representation of a fight she had not yet won, but not yet lost.

A scar to remember both the hurt that had been thrust upon her, and the hurt that she had thrust upon herself.

What's Left in the Middle.

5:15pm

And he said,

"Listen sunshine,   gray is not the
enemy."

Do you Play Piano?

8:36pm

I want you to play me a song I know.

No longer will I tolerate listening to your hearts disastrous notes collected in sharp, unforgiving tunes.

Just once, will your lungs play me something familiar?

Do you dare be benevolent and play me something to please my ears?

Timing.

In what tense: past or present? Future?

That's the funny thing about timing….. It has no sense of time. It rummages through life like an old friend you hardly keep in touch with, reminding you what you lost.

It sits next to you on the bus, so unassuming with headphones and straight posture.

It runs ahead of you, disappearing by the bend as you cringe, waiting for it to sprint into view again.

Timing. You unforgiving fool.

Weightless

2:21am

My love bears the weight of an eyelash through the wind; misplaced and unnoticed.

Have I told you lately?

11:07pm

I just wanted to let you know….

That the cobwebs in the corner have fell flat and disconnected.

The wails of woe have been trapped in the walls, they will sing no longer.

I just wanted to let you know….

You have illuminated my future by extinguishing my past and that is the greatest accomplishment thus far.

I just wanted to let you know.

Greasy Hands

1:00am

My brain is so trained to let things go that I no longer remember what it feels like to tightly grasp my fingers around something with permanence.

I Wear Tens.

7:34pm

"Try walking in someone else's shoes for once."

He replies, "But why? Mine have always fit just fine."

I trip behind him.

Good Cop, Bad Cop?

12:05am

How can I blame you for stealing from me if I gave you myself so willingly? You were a thief. Subconsciously you took, but only attributable to my willingness to give.

I cannot sit back and call myself a victim of your games when I so freely signed the contract to play.

I cannot call you a shoplifter of my fruit when I so eagerly gave you the basket. Seems as though I ended up robbing myself.

Bleed

1:25am

No longer do I want to hide from pain; suppressing it and suffocating it until it dies inside me. I want to feel it, be it, and unfreeze myself from it. I want to call it on a Friday night and go to dinner with it.

Maybe we'll catch a movie together. I want to dive inward and bathe in it, instead of swim outward and run from it. I want to bleed from it. I will deal with it. And through this process, I will heal in it.

Pretty Green Gazers

3:14pm

Expanding the definition of your worth is up to **you.** Learn to see yourself through the eyes which stare back at you every day. It is the most organic way you can ever begin to move forward in life.

Your Intuition

11:20pm

Keep up with the natural flow of your river, but do not be afraid to stop and listen to the water quietly splashing the side of your canoe. Your river is speaking to you. Your life is speaking to you.

If you keep floating on with arrogance, these small splashes will surely turn to a tidal wave. Listen before the river gets angry.

What I Want and What I Need

12:48am

I once wanted something so bad I was willing to lose myself for it. Willing to be bashed in the head with a brick for it. Willing to get the wind knocked out of me for it.

Letting someone steal my breath, only to return it poisoned with lies from their venomous soul.

Take it back. I'd rather suffocate than inhale such dangerous mistruths.

Welcome

1:54am

I am mourning the loss of my youth. This sparkling young girl, with nothing to lose.

But I am also celebrating the birth of a woman who no longer sparkles, but rather *glistens.*

To Hike a Steep Trail

3:30am

I do not regret any connections I've made with people, even if they turned out to be toxic and lethal. I do not pretend I haven't thought about regretting them, for that idea has permanently weighted my pillow at night.

However, there came a time when I saw my list of failed connections as a trail. A cast of shadowy footprints creeping behind me, made by friends turned strangers. A muddy trail which taught me something specific and unique in every footprint. Each a journey to lead to the next.

Don't find me mistaken, I do recognize the footsteps beside me and look to my left with gratitude. However, it's the ghostly impressions behind me, hardened and crusted with time in the mud, which allowed my soul to welcome the footprints next to mine with ease.

Crazy Kids

9:39pm

When I was young, I wished to live forever. How naïve. How despicable it would be to never experience the rarity of a moment and be cursed with the capacity to repeat.

These days, that very repetition is what I run from.

Chaos

10:59pm

For I have always been more comfortable with the booming roar of a lion between my ears; much preferred over the "baaaing" of a sheep.

I get better sleep this way.

In Regards to, "How have you been?"
7:38am

Steady catching rain from the sun, running from fires in the wind and carrying a thousand ton elephant up a spiral staircase. How about yourself?

My Wounded Mind

5:55pm

A muddled blood bath of fiery strife. Wounded cries from the North echo the empty spaces in the South. Gunshots blaring, soldiers falling....

I'm interrupted.

"What's for dinner?"

False Utopia

12:34am

Be wary of something that feels too good to be true.

Remember that the sun will burn you to an absolute crisp if you bask in it for too long. It is okay to take shade every now and then, my dear.

I've Made a Mistake

10:00am

I have been trained to associate feelings with an object outside my being. From a young age, I would feel happy standing by the ocean, or receiving a new toy for Christmas. Now, when I stand by the ocean, I am still flooded with joy and nostalgia of my youth.

And while it is delightful to associate the smell of freshly baked cookies with grandma's house, what happens when that associated feeling is stolen from an outside source?

See, I once gave away my feeling of joy to a boy. I still see our shadows towering in the subtle light of a streetlamp. But when he left, I no longer had that joy. It was given to him.

I guess what I am trying to say is that feelings belong to you. They stem from an inward eruption of your soul. They are not to be owned or given to an outside source. Remember that. Your feelings are mixed up inside you. Never forget that YOU have the power to save those emotions from thieves.

Blurred Lines

1:26am

When it comes to love, the lines are not blurred at all. The lines are dark scratches, sketched with black marker. Completely opaque.

Dense.

Completely impenetrable.

Come Down from Your Tower

I figured out why we put people on a pedestal after they're gone.

It is because they no longer have the opportunity to let us down.

They can stay up high and it's guaranteed   that when they're gone, they cannot be lowered anymore.

When someone is out of our lives, they no longer have the power to hurt us.

Of course   everyone seems better when they are gone!

Lessons and Love

1:04am

I think I have fallen in love with learning. Maybe that explains why I choose to love people who are wrong for me.

They are mistakes, leading to lessons. Lessons I'm addicted to learning over and over again.

Curtain Call

2:00am

The curtain has closed. Now, my darling, go pick up those roses at your feet.

Dream Big

1:13pm

I am on a steady path to the stars. I'm confidently moving towards my dreams. I'm living the life I've always imagined. I have myself to thank.

In the End,

3:30pm

All in all, I wish to change nothing.

For my mouth would not be able to taste the divine harmonies of the sweet sugars and lush caramels of this world, if my tongue wasn't first drenched in thirst-quenching salt.

ACKNOWLEDGMENTS

Writing this book has taken place because of a multitude of different precursors. Many people have played a role in bringing my vulnerable thoughts to light. For those of you who inspired these poems, I thank you for helping me find myself. Thank you, Victoria and Scott J. Prendergast, for standing by my side through everything in my life. Thank you, Herbert Byam, for editing some of my poems and displaying faith in me. Finally, thank you to Lisa and Scott M. Prendergast for inspiring me, reminding me that I am special, and prompting me to do anything I set my mind too.

I am blessed by those in my life; both those who made a wonderful impact on me, and those who left me broken. For better or worse, I thank anyone who touched my life in some way. You shaped me into the person that I am today. Thank you all for your support. I am truly blessed.